BOB ROZEMA

HC and ME

The Heidelberg Catechism for Christian Living

FAITH ALIVE®
Christian Resources

Grand Rapids, Michigan

CONTENTS

1 Q. **What is your only comfort
in life and in death?**[1]

A. That I am not my own,[1]
but belong—
body and soul,
in life and in death—[2]
to my faithful Savior Jesus Christ.[3]

He has fully paid for all my sins with his precious blood,[4]
and has set me free from the tyranny of the devil.[5]
He also watches over me in such a way[6]
that not a hair can fall from my head
without the will of my Father in heaven:[7]
in fact, all things must work together for my salvation.[8]

Because I belong to him,
Christ, by his Holy Spirit,
assures me of eternal life[9]
and makes me wholeheartedly willing and ready
from now on to live for him.[10]

[1] 1 Cor. 6:19-20
[2] Rom. 14:7-9
[3] 1 Cor. 3:23; Titus 2:14
[4] 1 Pet. 1:18-19; 1 John 1:7-9; 2:2
[5] John 8:34-36; Heb. 2:14-15; 1 John 3:1-11
[6] John 6:39-40; 10:27-30; 2 Thess. 3:3; 1 Pet. 1:5
[7] Matt. 10:29-31; Luke 21:16-18
[8] Rom. 8:28
[9] Rom. 8:15-16; 2 Cor. 1:21-22; 5:5; Eph. 1:13-14
[10] Rom. 8:1-17

THE BOTTOM LINE

<Warm-up>

Stresses. Everybody's got 'em. School is going OK until you get huge assignments in every subject just before your term paper is due; you're getting along with mom and dad until that big clash over what time you have to be home on Saturday night. And so on. With a partner, act out a stressful situation—at home, school, work, anywhere —that makes you want to go "Ahhhhhhhhhhhhhhhh!" You can be funny or serious or both. Keep it short (a minute or less).

Huguenots wore this cross as a sign of their faith.

Murder in Church

It's no accident that the Catechism begins with comfort. When the authors of the Catechism sat down to write in 1562, they had just received reports that dozens of Huguenots—French followers of John Calvin—had been slaughtered while worshiping in church. Their attackers—a group of French Catholics—killed sixty Huguenots and wounded two hundred more. In the years that followed, some ten thousand Huguenots died for their faith. Torture was common: men were usually burned at the stake; women were buried alive.

<Main Event>

1. When people are hurting, where are some of the places they look for comfort and help?

5

2. Underline what the Catechism says is our *only* comfort. What do you think it means when it says that this is our *only* comfort?

3. Look up the Scripture passages under the first three footnotes to Q&A 1. Find a phrase in each passage that says we belong to Jesus.

4. Privately remember a time when you especially needed God's comfort and strength (or imagine such a time in the future). Then circle one thing in answer 1 that would give you comfort and hope and strength in such a situation.

\<Follow-up\>

True comfort is not a strong hand we can cling to when life's storms or death's floods sweep over our heads. It is a powerful hand that holds onto us with a grip that nothing can break. Comfort is Christ's holding on to us when we lack the strength to hold on to him. We know his power is greater than ours—greater than the devil's or death's—and that he will never let us go. We belong to him. *That's* our true comfort.

How do you react to this picture of comfort?
- ☐ I can see it clearly and know in my heart that it's true.
- ☐ I sometimes feel I'm holding on to Jesus, not vice-versa.
- ☐ I haven't felt much of "life's storms" so I really don't know what to make of this.
- ☐ I want to believe this but sometimes find it difficult.
- ☐ I'm living with the joy and security of knowing I belong to Jesus.
- ☐ Right now, I don't see how any of this relates to my life.
- ☐ Other: _____

2 Q. **What must you know**
to live and die in the joy of this comfort?

A. Three things:
first, how great my sin and misery are;[1]
second, how I am set free from all my sins and misery;[2]
third, how I am to thank God for such deliverance.[3]

[1] Rom. 3:9-10; 1 John 1:10
[2] John 17:3; Acts 4:12; 10:43
[3] Matt. 5:16; Rom. 6:13; Eph. 5:8-10; 2 Tim. 2:15; 1 Pet. 2:9-10

HOW TO BE HAPPY

<Warm-up>

How do you think the "average person" would rank these common ingredients of being happy?

__ being smart
__ having lots of money
__ having a good job
__ being attractive
__ having good health
__ having a loving family
__ being famous (as in sports or entertainment)
__ believing in God and belonging to a church
__ having lots of friends
__ being content
__ other: _____
__ other: _____

<Main Event>

Misery (Sin)

Read Romans 3:9-12 and the first line of answer 2.

1. If you were an artist who wanted to illustrate human misery, what might you sketch? Make a simple drawing or just describe your sketch in words. Or, if you prefer, pantomime how people feel when they suddenly realize they've messed up big-time.

2. "To know real joy in God, [we need to] know inside and out, up and down, through and through, how full of sin we are. We're just fooling ourselves if we think we're without sin. And that's not easy for any-one to confess. Nobody wants to look bad" (*Every Bit of Who I Am,* p. 17). What do you think the Catechism means about *knowing* how great our sin and misery are, and why is that necessary?

3. What does this part of answer 2 tell us we need to experience on a day-to-day basis?

4. What Q&A's are included in the Misery (Sin) section of the Catechism?

Deliverance (Salvation)

Read Romans 5:6-9 and the second line of answer 2.

1. If you were an artist who wanted to illustrate deliverance from sin, what might you sketch? Make a simple drawing or just describe your sketch in words. Or, if you prefer, pantomime how people feel when they realize they've been forgiven for doing something pretty awful.

2. What do you think the Catechism means about *knowing* how we are set free from our sin and misery? What exactly do we need to know?

3. What does this part of answer 2 tell us we need to experience on a day-to-day basis?

4. What Q&A's are included in the Deliverance (Salvation) section of the Catechism? What creed is explained in this section?

Gratitude (Service)

Read Romans 12:1 and the third line of answer 2.

1. If you were an artist who wanted to illustrate a life of gratitude and service, what might you sketch? Make a simple drawing or describe your sketch in words. Or, if you prefer, pantomime what a life of gratitude and service might look like.

2. What do you think the Catechism means about *knowing* how we are to thank God for our deliverance? What does the Catechism mean by *know*? According to the Catechism, what would our motivation be for taking time to help out a neighbor or friend?

3. What does this part of answer 2 tell us we need to experience on a day-to-day basis?

4. What Q&A's are included in the Gratitude (Service) part of the Catechism? What prayer is found there? What guide to Christian living?

\<Follow-up\>

You are invited to complete the statements to form a prayer asking God to let you live the joy of knowing you belong to him.

(Sin) Loving God, I admit that I

_____

_____.

(Salvation) Loving God, I celebrate the way you

_____

_____.

(Service) Loving God, in response to what you have done for me, I want to

_____

_____.

Amen.

3 Q. How do you come to know your misery?
A. The law of God tells me.[1]

[1] Rom. 3:20; 7:7-25

4 Q. What does God's law require of us?
A. Christ teaches us this in summary in Matthew 22 —

Love the Lord your God
with all your heart
and with all your soul
and with all your mind
and with all your strength.[1*]
This is the first and greatest commandment.

And the second is like it:
Love your neighbor as yourself.[2]

All the Law and the Prophets hang
on these two commandments.

[1] Deut. 6:5
[2] Lev. 19:18
* Earlier and better manuscripts of Matthew 22 omit the words
"and with all your strength." They are found in Mark 12:30.

5 Q. Can you live up to all this perfectly?
A. No.[1]
I have a natural tendency
to hate God and my neighbor.[2]

[1] Rom. 3:9-20, 23; 1 John 1:8, 10
[2] Gen. 6:5; Jer. 17:9; Rom. 7:23-24; 8:7; Eph. 2:1-3; Titus 3:3

WHAT WE CAN'T DO

<Warm-Up>

Make up three action statements about yourself. Two of them should be true statements about things you're pretty good at ("I'm a decent downhill skier") and one should be false ("I can speed-read my way through a book in two or three hours flat"). Your classmates will be asked to guess which statement is false, so try not to make it too obvious!

<Main Event>

Read Q&A 3-5.

1. What does the Catechism say human beings just can't do? What predicament are we in? What word does the Catechism use to describe our condition because of this?

2. What does you think it means to be "in misery" because of our inability to do what God wants us to do? How does the law help us to discover our true condition?

3. Make a list of a dozen actions or attitudes that God requires of us in, say, an ordinary day. Make your list as specific as you can. You may include negatives (things to avoid) as well as positives (things to do).

4. The Catechism says that we "have a natural tendency to hate God and [our] neighbor." In my opinion,

- ☐ this applies only to people who aren't Christians.
- ☐ this simply isn't true of me or most people I know.
- ☐ this is hard to admit, but I sometimes can see that tendency to hate in my own life.
- ☐ this doesn't agree with what the Bible teaches about us being made in God's image.
- ☐ other:_____

Before you answer, please check out these Scripture passages: Romans 3:23-24; 1 John 1:8-10; Romans 7:18-24; Titus 3:3-7.

\<Follow-up\>

When do you tend to feel distant from God?

- ☐ when I'm feeling down
- ☐ when something bad happens in our world, like a huge earthquake or hurricane
- ☐ when something bad happens to a family member or friend
- ☐ when I've failed to acknowledge that I'm a Christian in a compromising situation
- ☐ when I've done something I know God doesn't approve of
- ☐ when something happens to me I feel I don't deserve
- ☐ other: _____

What helps you feel closer to God again?

- ☐ praying
- ☐ reading the Bible
- ☐ talking with a friend or family member
- ☐ honestly admitting to God that I'm wrong and need forgiveness
- ☐ realizing that God is there for me, no matter how I feel
- ☐ other: _____

Nobody's purfect!

6 Q. **Did God create people**
    so wicked and perverse?
  A. No.
    God created them good[1] and in his own image,[2]
        that is, in true righteousness and holiness,[3]
    so that they might
        truly know God their creator,[4]
        love him with all their heart,
        and live with him in eternal happiness
    for his praise and glory.[5]

[1] Gen. 1:31
[2] Gen. 1:26-27
[3] Eph. 4:24
[4] Col. 3:10
[5] Ps. 8

DON'T BLAME GOD

<Warm-up>

The Blame Game

OK, most of us occasionally play this game, which basically involves blaming someone else when we goof up. For example, when your teacher asks why you missed the deadline for turning in your paper, you say your other teachers gave you too much homework so you couldn't get the paper done in time. With a partner, think of a common "blame someone or something else" situation, then act it out for the class.

<Main Event>

1. Who or what might people blame for the misery and mess in our world (poverty, crime, terrorism, war, racism, greed, pollution, drug abuse, child abuse, hurricanes, earthquakes, and so on)?

2. Give an example of how you personally might blame God for something.

3. Underline the part of answer 6 that says why we shouldn't blame God for our misery.

4. What do you find in Genesis 1:26-32 that tells you God did not make people "wicked and perverse"?

5. Being made in the image of God suggests that people resemble God in who they are and what they do. In Genesis 1:26-32 and Ephesians 4:24, how did people resemble God in who they were and what they were like? How did they resemble God in what they did?

6. According to answer 6, what three things did God create people to do? What would be the result of doing these three things?

7. Have people today completely lost the image of God? Why or why not?

8. Read 2 Corinthians 5:17 and Ephesians 4:24. If we love and serve the Lord, what's happening to the image of God in us? How could this affect the way we see ourselves, especially when we're down on ourselves? The way we see other people? Our attitude toward the obvious sin and misery in our world?

\<Follow-up\>

If all this talk about "image of God" means anything, each person in your class actually reflects some of the goodness and holiness of God. This means we should be able to see something of God in each other! Your teacher will pass around cards. On each card write a classmate's name and something you really appreciate about him or her—either something about who he or she is or what he or she does.

Every Last One

"Think of the kid most despised by all your friends. Think of the kid you walk away from when school is over. Think of the kid you wouldn't date if it were just the two of you on earth. Then remember this: each one resembles God. That makes every last one of us loveable, every last one valuable and important. . . . Every last one of us looks something like God."

—James C. Schaap, *Every Bit of Who I Am*, page 20

7 Q. **Then where does this corrupt human nature come from?**

A. From the fall and disobedience of our first parents, Adam and Eve, in Paradise.[1]
This fall has so poisoned our nature[2]
that we are born sinners—
corrupt from conception on.[3]

[1] Gen. 3
[2] Rom. 5:12, 18-19
[3] Ps. 51:5

8 Q. **But are we so corrupt that we are totally unable to do any good and inclined toward all evil?**

A. Yes,[1] unless we are born again, by the Spirit of God.[2]

[1] Gen. 6:5; 8:21; Job 14:4; Isa. 53:6
[2] John 3:3-5

WHAT WENT WRONG?

\<Warm-up\>

■ Think of one event or person in human history that, for you, captures the meaning of human goodness and decency.
■ Think of one event or person in human history that, for you, captures the meaning of human evil or depravity.

\<Main Event\>

Beliefs About Sin

Working with a partner, put a check by the statements with which you agree. If you can't agree or don't understand a statement, put a question mark by it.

1. ☐ a. God created people and is ultimately to blame for the sins we commit and suffer from.
   ☐ b. God created people good and cannot be blamed for the sins we commit and suffer from.

2. ☐ a. Our sin began with Adam and Eve.
   ☐ b. Our sin begins with us whenever we do something wrong.

3. ☐ a. Infants are born sinful.
   ☐ b. Infants are born innocent, free from all sin.

4. ☐ a. We become sinners when we commit sins.
   ☐ b. We sin because we are sinners.

5. ☐ a. All people are sinners
   ☐ b. Some people are sinners.

6. ☐ a. All people are as bad as they can be.
   ☐ b. All people are affected by sin in every area of their lives.

7. ☐ a. Followers of Christ are capable of doing good and becoming better people.
   ☐ b. Followers of Christ, though saved, are still not capable of doing anything that is good in God's sight.

\<Follow-up\>

Working with a partner, depict with paper and markers—as imaginatively as you can—how the saving power of God's salvation in Christ breaks the power of sin in our lives.

Plunging into Sin—and Loving It

"Let's face the truth. There are times when even redeemed people purposely plunge themselves into sin. In fact, we use a diving board. We go in head first, eyes wide open. We *commit* sin. And we often like it. . . . Sometimes we even take pride in a particular sin and try to defend it. Can any one of us honestly say he or she has never relished a put-down of another human being—and then defended it on the ground that the person 'had it coming?'"

—Cornelius Plantinga, Jr., *Beyond Doubt,* page 146

9 Q. **But doesn't God do us an injustice**
by requiring in his law
what we are unable to do?

A. No, God created humans with the ability to keep the law.[1]
They, however, tempted by the devil,[2]
in reckless disobedience,[3]
robbed themselves and all their descendants of these gifts.[4]

[1] Gen. 1:31; Eph. 4:24
[2] Gen. 3:13; John 8:44
[3] Gen. 3:6
[4] Rom. 5:12, 18, 19

10 Q. **Will God permit**
such disobedience and rebellion
to go unpunished?

A. Certainly not.
He is terribly angry
about the sin we are born with
as well as the sins we personally commit.

As a just judge
he punishes them now and in eternity.[1]

He has declared:
"Cursed is everyone who does not continue to do
everything written in the Book of the Law."[2]

[1] Ex. 34:7; Ps. 5:4-6; Nah. 1:2; Rom. 1:18; Eph. 5:6; Heb. 9:27
[2] Gal. 3:10; Deut. 27:26

11 Q. **But isn't God also merciful?**

A. God is certainly merciful,[1]
but he is also just.[2]
His justice demands
that sin, committed against his supreme majesty,
be punished with the supreme penalty—
eternal punishment of body and soul.[3]

[1] Ex. 34:6-7; Ps. 103:8-9
[2] Ex. 34:7; Deut. 7:9-11; Ps. 5:4-6; Heb. 10:30-31
[3] Matt. 25:35-46

IS GOD LIKE THIS?

<Warm-up>

Here's kind of an off-the-wall question for you: How do you see God? Or, to put it another way, what is God like to you? Do any pictures come to mind, maybe an image from a Bible story or just something you see when you think about God? Try sketching your idea and maybe giving it a caption. If no picture comes to mind, just list some words that describe how you see God.

<Main Event>

Group 1

Read Q&A 9

◼ What wrong picture of God does question 9 suggest we might have? Why would we have this impression?

◼ According to answer 9, why is this impression or picture of God inaccurate? Look up and read (from the list in answer 9) one Bible passage that shows why this impression is wrong.

◼ If you were drawing an accurate picture of God based on answer 9, what would you draw?

Group 2

Read Q&A 10

◼ If you were drawing a picture of God based on this Q&A, what would you draw?

◼ Why does God feel this way, since every single human being sins all the time? Why is our sin such a big deal to God?

◼ How are some of our sins punished *now*? Give some examples.

◼ Look up and read one Bible passage (listed in answer 10) that supports this picture of God.

Group 3
Read Q&A 11

- If you were drawing a picture of God based on this Q&A, what would you draw?
- Look up and read one passage (listed in answer 11) that shows God is merciful.
- Look up and read one passage (listed in answer 11) that shows God is just.
- How does God's justice in punishing sin also show God's mercy and love?

<Follow-up>

Reflect quietly on this:

> If God were only a judge, we could count on hell for sure. But we do not begin our prayers "Your Honor," but simply "Our Father." In Hosea 11, this Father asks his people, "How can I give you up?" And the answer is in the gospel: "I will not give you up at all. I'll give up another. . . . For unto you is born this day in the city of David, a Savior, who is Christ the Lord."

Then take a moment to say a silent prayer telling God how you feel about your sin and what God has done to save you from it.

12 Q. According to God's righteous judgment
we deserve punishment
both in this world and forever after:
how then can we escape this punishment
and return to God's favor?

Why do we deserve
punishment?

Why does God
require this?

How can we escape
God's punishment
for our sin?

A. God requires that his justice be satisfied.
Therefore the claims of his justice
must be paid in full,
either by ourselves or another.

Go around the circle
and name some
ways we might try to
pay the debt of our
sin ourselves.

On a separate sheet of
paper, describe a time
when you felt guilty
and how you tried to
get rid of your guilt.
(Not for sharing.)

13 Q. Can we pay this debt ourselves?

A. Certainly not.
Actually, we increase our guilt every day.

Go around the circle
and name some ways
we deal with our guilt
(try to get rid of it).
What works for you?
What doesn't?

14 Q. Can another creature—any at all—
pay this debt for us?

A. No.
To begin with,
God will not punish another creature
for what a human is guilty of.
Besides,
no mere creature can bear the weight
of God's eternal anger against sin
and release others from it.

What abuses in the
Catholic church of
the Middle Ages do
you think the
Catechism writers
were concerned
about in Q&A 13-14?

What's a mediator?
Why do we need one?

15 Q. What kind of mediator and deliverer
should we look for then?

A. One who is truly human and truly righteous,
yet more powerful than all creatures,
that is, one who is also true God.

Imagine yourself
owing a huge debt
to someone, a debt
you have absolutely
no chance whatso-
ever to pay. Then
someone comes
along and says he
or she will pay
back the debt for
you and you're off
the hook for good.
In this Q&A, the
Catechism is
pointing us toward
the only One who
can pay our debt to
God. On a separate
sheet of paper,
write a short prayer
expressing how you
feel about what this
Savior is prepared
to do for you.

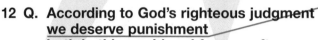
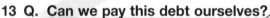

PAY UP!

<Warm-up>

Check the stuff that you'd be willing to go into debt for right now or in the next few years (just put down what you think—there are no right or wrong answers):

- ☐ great clothes
- ☐ cell phone
- ☐ music and equipment to play it
- ☐ concerts
- ☐ a really great Christmas present for my girlfriend/boyfriend/kid brother
- ☐ help family during hard times (unemployment, sickness)
- ☐ donation for hurricane or earthquake victims
- ☐ church
- ☐ sports stuff
- ☐ car (and insurance, gas, and repairs)
- ☐ college education or vocational training
- ☐ my own place
- ☐ other: _____
- ☐ other: _____

Now try some real speculation: at the ripe old age of 21, I expect to be

- ☐ debt-free and saving money
- ☐ mildly in debt, like say $_____
- ☐ deeply in debt, like say $_____
- ☐ rich, like say, worth about $_____

<Main Event>

Work through Q&A 12-15 with your group, pausing as indicated to

 discuss a question with the whole group whenever you see this symbol

 go around the circle with each person responding whenever you see this symbol

 write a private response on a separate piece of paper whenever you see this symbol

<Follow-up>

A wonderful passage that focuses on how Christ took our place is Isaiah 53:1-6. Pick a phrase from that passage about Jesus taking our place, then say that phrase to the rest of the class.

Money in the Box

"The minute you hear your money drop into the box, the soul of your relative will jump out of purgatory."

—Tetzel, selling "indulgences" to believers. His abuses led Martin Luther to write his ninety-five theses and nail them to the door of the Castle church in Wittenburg on October 31, 1517 —thus beginning the Protestant Reformation.

**16 Q. Why must he be truly human
and truly righteous?**

A. God's justice demands
that human nature, which has sinned,
must pay for its sin;[1]
but a sinner could never pay for others.[2]

[1] Rom. 5:12, 15; 1 Cor. 15:21; Heb. 2:14-16
[2] Heb. 7:26-27; 1 Pet. 3:18

17 Q. Why must he also be true God?

A. So that,
by the power of his divinity,
he might bear the weight of God's anger in his humanity
and earn for us
and restore to us
righteousness and life.[1]

[1] Isa. 53; John 3:16; 2 Cor. 5:21

**18 Q. And who is this mediator—
true God and at the same time
truly human and truly righteous?**

A. Our Lord Jesus Christ,[1]
who was given us
to set us completely free
and to make us right with God.[2]

[1] Matt. 1:21-23; Luke 2:11; 1 Tim. 2:5
[2] 1 Cor. 1:30

19 Q. How do you come to know this?

A. The holy gospel tells me.
God himself began to reveal the gospel already in Paradise;[1]
later, he proclaimed it
by the holy patriarchs[2] and prophets,[3]
and portrayed it
by the sacrifices and other ceremonies of the law;[4]
finally, he fulfilled it
through his own dear Son.[5]

[1] Gen. 3:15
[2] Gen. 22:18; 49:10
[3] Isa. 53; Jer. 23:5-6; Mic. 7:18-20; Acts 10:43; Heb. 1:1-2
[4] Lev. 1-7; John 5:46; Heb. 10:1-10
[5] Rom. 10:4; Gal. 4:4-5; Col. 2:17

OUR BROTHER, OUR SAVIOR

\<Warm-up\>

Pick a Bible story that you most often think about when thinking of Jesus. It can be a favorite story or one that helps you or comforts you in some way or that says something else to you. Describe your story on a card or slip of paper (in just a title or line) and see if you can find one other person in the class who chose the same story. Stand with that person when/if you find him or her. If you can't find a match, that's OK.

\<Main Event\>

1. With a partner, jot down (on one side of a separate sheet of paper) why it's important for us to know and believe that Jesus is human. On the other side of the paper, jot down why it's important to know and believe that Jesus is divine (God). Please don't refer to the Catechism when writing. Use your own thoughts and words.

2. Read Q&A 18 and the quote from James Schaap on pages 36-37. Underline something from the Q&A or from the quote that you find especially meaningful, helpful, or thought-provoking.

3. Read Q&A 19. Behind each Old Testament passage on the diagram, write in the New Testament fulfillment from the passages listed below.
   - Hebrews 13:11-12
   - Mark 10:45
   - Hebrews 2:14
   - Galatians 3:14

Old Testament Preparation ・ New Testament Fulfillment

B.C. Paradise/Genesis 3:15

Patriarchs/Genesis 12:3

2000 B.C.

Law/Leviticus 16:17

Prophets/Isaiah 53:11

1300 B.C.

800 B.C.

<Follow-up>

Notice how answer 19 turns very personal: "the gospel tells *me.*"
We invite you to do one of the following:

■ Write a short statement about what you believe about Jesus
Christ (or jot down questions or issues you may have).

■ Write (or draw) about how Jesus is present in your life today (or
how you would like him to be present).

■ Describe one of the key ways that you've come to know Jesus or
to know him better.

■ Describe (or draw) a special or difficult time in your life when you
strongly felt Jesus was with you.

■ Choose a song that expresses your feelings about Jesus. You
don't have to sing it but be ready to explain why you chose it.

You'll be asked to share your responses with the group, if you wish
to do so.

Nobody Like Him

"How can a God—a being beyond time and space, someone
who knew your great-great-great-great grandparents as well as
you—how can such a God be a hiccupping, nose-blowing,
putty-bellied man?

Did you ever hear of a person who was half chicken? How about
half fern? Humans are humans, right? You can't mix a human being
with an organ-pipe cactus or a Rhesus monkey. It's impossible.

Well, so is the man/God Jesus Christ. You may have heard of him since you were knee-high, but if you don't think of him as the most astounding miracle, then you really don't know him. He's human, like us—and he's God. Both at once.

There's nobody like him and never has been. And, get this, he loves us."

—James C. Schaap, *Every Bit of Who I Am,* page 32

20 Q. Are all saved through Christ just as all were lost through Adam?

A. No.
Only those are saved
who by true faith
    are grafted into Christ
    and accept all his blessings.[1]

[1] Matt. 7:14; John 3:16, 18, 36; Rom. 11:16-21

21 Q. What is true faith?

A. True faith is
    not only a knowledge and conviction
        that everything God reveals in his Word is true;[1]
    it is also a deep-rooted assurance,[2]
        created in me by the Holy Spirit[3] through the gospel,[4]
        that, out of sheer grace earned for us by Christ,[5]
            not only others, but I too,[6]
                have had my sins forgiven,
                have been made forever right with God,
                and have been granted salvation.[7]

[1] John 17:3, 17; Heb. 11:1-3; James 2:19
[2] Rom. 4:18-21; 5:1; 10:10; Heb. 4:14-16
[3] Matt. 16:15-17; John 3:5; Acts 16:14
[4] Rom. 1:16; 10:17; 1 Cor. 1:21
[5] Rom. 3:21-26; Gal. 2:16; Eph. 2:8-10
[6] Gal. 2:20
[7] Rom. 1:17; Heb. 10:10

I BELIEVE

<Warm-up>

We live by faith. Keep that in mind as you complete these statements:

■ If I'm driving right behind a huge earthmover chained to a truck going seventy miles an hour, I need faith that

_____.

■ If I'm handing in a term paper to a teacher at school, I need faith that

_____.

■ If I'm sharing a secret with a friend, I need faith that

_____.

■ If I'm sneaking into the house after curfew, I need faith that

_____.

■ If . . . *(fill in your own example of faith)*

_____.

<Main Event (Read Q&A 21)>

1. Underline the part of answer 21 that says you need "head knowledge" to have faith. What do you need to *know* and be convinced of?

2. Circle the part of answer 21 that says you also need "heart knowledge" to have faith. What do you need to *feel* assured of? If you're willing, share with the group a time when you really felt convinced of these things, when your faith was especially strong and alive.

3. How do we get true faith?

4. Which of the following do you agree with?
   - ☐ Having doubts is a sign of a sick faith or no faith.
   - ☐ Most Christians have doubts at one time or another.

5. When/if you have doubts about what you believe or about God in general, how do you deal with these feelings? What in answer 21 could help you during times of doubt?

\<Follow-up\>

Hebrews 11 describes some of the champions of faith from the Old Testament. Then, in Hebrews 12:1-3, we're told that all these heroes of faith are like a crowd in a grandstand, watching us and cheering us on as we run our race of faith. Think about your own "race of faith" and where you are in it:

- ☐ I'm running, but I'd like to *know* more about the race and the One I should keep my eyes fixed on.
- ☐ I'm running, but I'd like to *feel* more assured that the race is worth running and that the goal is worth all the effort.
- ☐ I'm running, stumbling sometimes and even doubting my ability to run, but keeping my eye on Jesus. I know for sure that I'll finish with him in glory.
- ☐ Right now, I'm tired of running and I've sort of given up on the race.
- ☐ I really haven't entered the race yet because I'm not sure if I'm ready.
- ☐ other :_____

Think about your response, then write a short prayer to Jesus expressing thanks for the faith he's given you and asking for help where you feel you most need it.

Get On with It

"Do you see what this means—all these pioneers who blazed the way, all these veterans cheering us on? It means we'd better get on with it. Strip down, start running—and never quit! . . . Keep your eye on *Jesus,* who both began and finished this race we're in. Study how he did it. Because he never lost sight of where he was headed . . . he could put up with anything along the way: cross, shame, whatever. And now he's *there,* in the place of honor, right alongside God. When you find yourself flagging in your faith, go over that story again, item by item. . . ."

—Hebrews 12:1-3, *The Message*

22 Q. What then must a Christian believe?

A. Everything God promises us in the gospel.[1]
That gospel is summarized for us
in the articles of our Christian faith—
a creed beyond doubt,
and confessed throughout the world.

[1] Matt. 28:18-20; John 20:30-31

23 Q. What are these articles?

A. I believe in God, the Father almighty,
creator of heaven and earth.

I believe in Jesus Christ, his only Son, our Lord,
who was conceived by the Holy Spirit
and born of the virgin Mary.
He suffered under Pontius Pilate,
was crucified, died, and was buried;
he descended to hell.
The third day he rose again from the dead.
He ascended to heaven
and is seated at the right hand of God the Father almighty.
From there he will come to judge the living and the dead.

I believe in the Holy Spirit,
the holy catholic church,
the communion of saints,
the forgiveness of sins,
the resurrection of the body,
and the life everlasting. Amen.

A CREED BEYOND DOUBT

<Warm-up>

Read Q&A 22. Write "True" or "False" by the following statements about the Apostles' Creed. (If you don't know, just take a guess. You've got a 50/50 chance of being right!)

1. ____ The word *creed* means "I believe."
2. ____ Jesus taught his disciples the Apostles' Creed.
3. ____ You can find the Apostles' Creed in the gospels of Matthew and John.
4. ____ The Creed was written around the time of the Reformation, mostly by Martin Luther.
5. ____ The creed is about 1,600 years old.
6. ____ Each apostle or disciple wrote one of the twelve parts of the Apostles' Creed.
7. ____ When the church began, persons who joined it were baptized using a simple form of the Apostles' Creed.
8. ____ The Apostles' Creed is organized around the three persons of the Trinity.
9. ____ Most of the Apostles' Creed is about God the Father.
10. ____ The Creed is often used as a confession of faith during worship services.
11. ____ The Creed is often used as a teaching tool as a reminder of what we believe.
12. ____ The Apostles' Creed is used only by Reformed and Presbyterian churches in North America.

Bonus question: Name the infamous unbeliever mentioned in the Apostles' Creed.

\<Main Event\>

1. Imagine that the Apostles' Creed does not exist and that you've been asked to write a creed for the church as you know it today. You should write what you believe to be true in your own words.
    - ■ Group 1: Write "we believe" statements about God the Father.
    - ■ Group 2: Write "we believe" statements about Jesus.
    - ■ Group 3: Write "we believe" statements about the Holy Spirit and the church.

2. One of the earliest creeds about Jesus is found in Philippians 2:5-11. Read this passage and then draw an arrow pointing down next to those lines of the Apostles' Creed that follow the pattern of verses 5-8. Draw an arrow pointing up next to those lines that follow the pattern of verses 9-11. How would you describe those patterns?

\<Follow-up\>

Please complete one or more of the following:
- ■ When I think about the Apostles' Creed, I wonder

_____

_____

_____

_____

- ■ The Creed could be useful in my own life to

_____

_____

_____

_____

■ One question I'd like to ask God or Jesus is

_____

_____

_____

If You Confess . . .

"If you confess with your mouth, 'Jesus is Lord,' and believe in your heart that God raised him from the dead, you will be saved."

—Romans 10:9

24 Q. How are these articles divided?

    A. Into three parts:

        God the Father and our creation;

        God the Son and our deliverance;

        God the Holy Spirit and our sanctification.

**25 Q. Since there is but one God,[1]
why do you speak of three:
Father, Son, and Holy Spirit?**

    A. Because that is how

        God has revealed himself in his Word:[2]

        these three distinct persons

        are one, true, eternal God.

[1] Deut. 6:4; 1 Cor. 8:4, 6

[2] Matt. 3:16-17; 28:18-19; Luke 4:18 (Isa. 61:1); John 14:26; 15:26; 2 Cor. 13:14; Gal. 4:6; Tit. 3:5-6

TRINITY

\<Warm-up\>

You will be asked to think about and worship our great and awesome God.

\<Main Event\>

Who God Is

1. Read Deuteronomy 6:4; 1 Corinthians 8:4; and Ephesians 4:4-6. Jot down the main idea about God that these passages show us.

2. Read Matthew 3:16-17; John 14:26; and 2 Corinthians 13:14. Jot down the main idea about God that these passages show us.

3. Now try combining in a single statement what the passages in items 1 and 2, above, say about God.

4. Underline the words from answer 25 that sum up what the Catechism says about God. Write the word "Trinity" next to these lines.

5. On a separate sheet of paper, work with others to draw or write something that attempts to explain the idea of the Trinity to someone your age. You may use a comparison (such as water in its three forms), pictures, words, or a combination of these. Give it your best shot.

6. Why believe in the Trinity when it's so difficult to explain and the word itself doesn't even appear in the Bible?

What God Does

7. Read Q&A 24. What "articles" are this question and question 23 talking about?

8. How are these twelve articles organized? What words start each section? Which section is the longest?

9. One way to describe God is by what God does, by his actions. Fill in the blanks to remind yourself of what God has done and is doing for you.

God has been and is at work in your life. For starters (literally), God the Father placed you in the beautiful world he _____. Even though that world has been spoiled by sin, and even though you were born tainted by sin, God the Father still made you in his _____ (Genesis 1:26). You are God's child and you _____ the One who made you!

But even God's children sin and are in need of _____. Because God the _____ loved the world and you so much, he _____ (John 3:16). By Christ's sacrifice on Calvary you are _____ from all your sin. God the _____ looks at you and sees only the _____ perfect obedience. The great work of God the Son is to be our _____. But even in heaven at the right hand of God the Father, the Son is _____ for you! (Romans 8:34). And he's busy preparing a _____ for you in heaven (John 14:3).

God the Son did not leave you and other believers alone on earth. He promised to always be with you! He keeps that promise every day through the work of God the Holy Spirit. The Spirit's work, called _____ (Q&A 24), helps you live as God wants you to live. The Spirit lives in your _____, guides you into all _____ (John 16:13), and gives you the strength and courage and vision you need to be a child of God.

Father, Son, and Spirit—one God who acts in three distinct ways. God created us, God delivered us, God sanctifies us. All to make sure that you <I>never<I> slip out of God's loving hands.

<Follow-up>

Think about how you might respond to the work of the Father, Son, and Holy Spirit in your life. Complete the statements below with something that you commit yourself to *doing* during the coming week.

■ Because God the Father created me and our world, I will

_____

■ Because God the Son died for me and saves me from all my sin, I will

_____

■ Because God the Holy Spirit is at work in me to make me more like Jesus, I will_____

_____

Billy Graham on the Trinity

"[The Trinity] is a terribly difficult subject—far beyond the ability of our limited minds to grasp fully. Nevertheless, it is extremely important to declare what the Bible holds, and be silent where the Bible is silent. God the Father is fully God. God the Son is fully God. God the Holy Spirit is fully God. The Bible presents this as fact. It does not explain it."

—Billy Graham, *The Faithful Christian: An Anthology of Billy Graham,* as quoted in *The Book of Jesus,* edited by Calvin Miller, page 69

**26 Q. What do you believe when you say,
"I believe in God, the Father almighty,
creator of heaven and earth"?**

A. That the eternal Father of our Lord Jesus Christ,
who out of nothing created heaven and earth
and everything in them,[1]
who still upholds and rules them
by his eternal counsel and providence,[2]
is my God and Father
because of Christ his Son.[3]

I trust him so much that I do not doubt
he will provide
whatever I need
for body and soul,[4]
and he will turn to my good
whatever adversity he sends me
in this sad world.[5]

He is able to do this because he is almighty God;[6]
he desires to do this because he is a faithful Father.[7]

[1] Gen. 1 & 2; Ex. 20:11; Ps. 33:6; Isa. 44:24; Acts 4:24; 14:15
[2] Ps. 104; Matt. 6:30; 10:29; Eph. 1:11
[3] John 1:12-13; Rom. 8:15-16; Gal. 4:4-7; Eph. 1:5
[4] Ps. 55:22; Matt. 6:25-26; Luke 12:22-31
[5] Rom. 8:28
[6] Gen. 18:14; Rom. 8:31-39
[7] Matt. 7:9-11

GOD OUR FATHER

\<Warm-up\>

Create a new life form using tin foil (it doesn't need to be life-size). It can be fish, fowl, mammal, microorganism, or anything at all. Place it on the blank side of the paper bag and draw its environment—where it lives, its food, its neighbors, its predators, and anything else you can think of that would be part of its web of life.

—Thea Nyhoff Leunk, *Fossils and Faith: Finding Our Way Through the Creation Controversy,*
Faith Alive Christian Resources

\<Main Event\>

Psalm 104

■ Read enough of Psalm 104 to give you a sense of what it says about God. Share with the group one or two verses and what you think they show about God. How do these verses make you feel about God?

■ Underline the part of Q&A 26 that describes this aspect of God.

■ What difference does it make whether we are created by God or live here as the result of some kind of chemical accident? What kinds of questions does believing in God as Creator *not* answer?

Luke 15:11-32

■ What does this parable tell you about God the Father?

■ Imagine yourself as the young person who sees his father running down the road to meet him, and who gets a huge hug from his dad. How does this parable make you feel about God the Father?

■ What's a huge surprise about God in Q&A 26 and in the contrast between Psalm 104 and the parable of the lost son?

■ According to Q&A 26 what two things can we trust God our Father to do for us? Why does he do it?

■ How much should we trust God? Is that hard or easy to do? Why?

<Follow-up>

■ The truths expressed in this Q&A have the power to touch our hearts and change our lives. What will you take with you from this session that could help you during the coming week and the rest of your life? Jot your thoughts below. You'll be invited to share them with one or two others, if you wish.

Soar Like Eagles

"Why would you ever complain . . . or whine . . . saying,
"God has lost track of me.
He doesn't care what happens to me"?
Don't you know anything? Haven't you been listening?
GOD doesn't come and go. God *lasts.*
He's Creator of all you can see or imagine.
He doesn't get tired out, doesn't pause to catch his breath.
and he knows *everything,* inside and out.
He energizes those who get tired,
gives fresh strength to dropouts.
For even young people tire and drop out,
young folks in their prime stumble and fall.
But those who wait upon GOD get fresh strength.
They spread their wings and soar like eagles.
They run and don't get tired,
they walk and don't lag behind."

—Isaiah 40:27-31, *The Message*

**27 Q. What do you understand
by the providence of God?**

A. Providence is
the almighty and ever present power of God[1]
by which he upholds, as with his hand,
heaven
and earth
and all creatures,[2]
and so rules them that
leaf and blade,
rain and drought,
fruitful and lean years,
food and drink,
health and sickness,
prosperity and poverty—[3]
all things, in fact, come to us
not by chance[4]
but from his fatherly hand.[5]

[1] Jer. 23:23-24; Acts 17:24-28
[2] Heb. 1:3
[3] Jer. 5:24; Acts 14:15-17; John 9:3; Prov. 22:2
[4] Prov. 16:33
[5] Matt. 10:29

**28 Q. How does the knowledge
of God's creation and providence
help us?**

A. We can be patient when things go against us,[1]
thankful when things go well,[2]
and for the future we can have
good confidence in our faithful God and Father
that nothing will separate us from his love.[3]
All creatures are so completely in his hand
that without his will
they can neither move nor be moved.[4]

[1] Job 1:21-22; James 1:3
[2] Deut. 8:10; 1 Thess. 5:18
[3] Ps. 55:22; Rom. 5:3-5; 8:38-39
[4] Job 1:12; 2:6; Prov. 21:1; Acts 17:24-28

GOD'S PROVIDENCE

<Warm-up>

Imagine that you're a famous artist and you've been commissioned by the Vatican to produce a painting that shows God's care and control of the world and its creatures. You are free to choose any subject you wish; a caption is allowed but not required. If you prefer, you may work with a partner. A rough draft of your painting is due soon (like in five minutes!). So what will you draw?

<Main Event>

1. Christians don't say "luck" or "chance" when explaining how they narrowly escaped an accident or how they met their spouse or how they get enough to eat every day. They give God the credit for such things. The fancy word for this is *providence.* Underline two verbs in answer 27 that tell what God in providence *does.* Think about what these words mean to you.

2. Suppose you wanted to point out to a non-Christian friend one way that God cares for you and/or the world. What might you mention?

3. If *all* things come from God's fatherly hand, does that mean that God caused terrorists to crash their planes into the World Trade Center towers and the Pentagon on 9/11? Does it mean that God causes cancer and other diseases, accidents, wars, poverty, tsunamis, and all the other crummy stuff that goes on in our world? Why or why not?

4. What should we say to people who look at tragedies in their personal lives or in the world at large and blame God?

5. Underline the three benefits of providence mentioned in answer 28. If you were explaining to someone how knowing about God's care and control of the world helps you, would you say the same thing as answer 28? Something different? Something additional?

6. What Bible passages or stories could help us remember that God will always love us and that nothing can separate us from that love?

\<Follow-up\>

1. Jot down a recent blessing for which you can thank God.

2. Jot down one concern about the future for which you especially need to trust God.

3. Choose one idea or image from Q&A 27-28 or from Scripture or our discussion that reassures or helps you in some way. Describe how that idea could make a difference in your week at school or at work or at home.

When Bad Things Happen

"You may never have hit bottom. You may never have been so low that looking up seemed downright impossible. . . . But, sorry as I am to say it, you probably will some time or other. . . . Bad things happen. . . . The shocking beauty of . . . providence is that even when things go entirely against us, we can be dead-on sure that God will be there with us. Nothing in all creation can ever separate us from God's love."

—James C. Schaap, *Every Bit of Who I Am,* page 63

**29 Q. Why is the Son of God called "Jesus,"
meaning "savior"?**

   A. Because he saves us from our sins.[1]
   Salvation cannot be found in anyone else;
   it is futile to look for any salvation elsewhere.[2]

   [1] Matt. 1:21; Heb. 7:25
   [2] Isa. 43:11; John 15:5; Acts 4:11-12; 1 Tim. 2:5

**30 Q. Do those who look for
their salvation and security
in saints, in themselves, or elsewhere
really believe in the only savior Jesus?**

   A. No.
   Although they boast of being his,
   by their deeds they deny
   the only savior and deliverer, Jesus.[1]

   Either Jesus is not a perfect savior,
   or those who in true faith accept this savior
   have in him all they need for their salvation.[2]

   [1] 1 Cor. 1:12-13; Gal. 5:4
   [2] Col. 1:19-20; 2:10; 1 John 1:7

WHY ARE YOU CALLED A CHRISTIAN?

\<Warm-up\>

What makes Christians different from other people? With others in your group, list as many *actions* as you can that could cause others to see something of Jesus in us and to realize that we are his followers.

\<Main Event\>

Q&A 29-30

1. Read through Q&A 29-30. Jot down all the things you can learn about Jesus from these questions and answers. Put an asterisk (*) by the one thing that's most important to believe about Jesus. What familiar Bible verse supports this key idea?

2. "Right now we're at the very heart of the gospel—Jesus saves us from our sins. Yawn. For many of us, that line has as much power as 'Have a nice day'" (James C. Schaap, *Every Bit of Who I Am*). Why might we sometimes feel this way? What helps you have a fresh appreciation of what Jesus has done for you?

3. Who did the Catechism writers likely have in mind when they wrote Q&A 30 back in the mid-1500s? What does Q&A 30 say about all the good *actions* that we listed earlier in the session?

31 Q. Why is he called "Christ,"
meaning "anointed"?

   A. Because he has been ordained by God the Father
     and has been anointed with the Holy Spirit[1]
        to be
        our chief prophet and teacher[2]
           who perfectly reveals to us
           the secret counsel and will of God for our deliverance;[3]
        our only high priest[4]
           who has set us free by the one sacrifice of his body,[5]
           and who continually pleads our cause with the Father;[6]
        and our eternal king[7]
           who governs us by his Word and Spirit,
           and who guards us and keeps us
           in the freedom he has won for us.[8]

[1] Luke 3:21-22; 4:14-19 (Isa. 61:1); Heb. 1:9 (Ps. 45:7)
[2] Acts 3:22 (Deut. 18:15)
[3] John 1:18; 15:15
[4] Heb. 7:17 (Ps. 110:4)
[5] Heb. 9:12; 10:11-14
[6] Rom. 8:34; Heb. 9:24
[7] Matt. 21:5 (Zech. 9:9)
[8] Matt. 28:18-20; John 10:28; Rev. 12:10-11

32 Q. But why are you called a Christian?

   A. Because by faith I am a member of Christ[1]
     and so I share in his anointing.[2]
        I am anointed
        to confess his name,[3]
        to present myself to him as a living sacrifice of thanks,[4]
        to strive with a good conscience against sin and the devil
           in this life,[5]
        and afterward to reign with Christ
           over all creation
           for all eternity.[6]

[1] 1 Cor. 12:12-27
[2] Acts 2:17 (Joel 2:28); 1 John 2:27
[3] Matt. 10:32; Rom. 10:9-10; Heb. 13:15
[4] Rom. 12:1; 1 Pet. 2:5, 9
[5] Gal. 5:16-17; Eph. 6:11; 1 Tim. 1:18-19
[6] Matt. 25:34; 2 Tim. 2:12

Q&A 31

4. If Jesus is our Lord's personal name (like our first names), how does the name "Christ" function?

5. When was Christ anointed? (see Luke 3:21-22). For what three roles or tasks?

6. Reflect on what Christ does as our prophet, priest, and king. How was Christ received as a prophet (see Luke 4:24, 28-30)? As a priest, how did Christ differ from Old Testament priests (see Isaiah 53:4-6)? What kind of king did Jesus turn out to be (see Matthew 20:28)?

Q&A 32

7. Notice how Q&A 32 switches from Christ to *us.* It says we are called Christian because we belong to Christ by faith. So how are we "anointed?" By whom?

8. Our job description as Christians matches that of Christ. Write "prophet," "priest," or "king" in front of the lines in answer 32 that you think describe each of these roles.

9. Mention at least three specific ways that we can
   - ◼ act as prophets and "confess Christ's name."
   - ◼ act as priests and present ourselves to God as "living sacrifices."
   - ◼ act as kings and fight against sin and evil?

Check out the actions we listed at the beginning of the session — things that cause others to see something of Jesus in us. You may use any items from that list that fit one or more of the above categories. Add some new items as well. For help, look up some of the passages listed in the footnotes to answer 32.

\<Follow-up\>

Q&A 32 is beautiful statement of faith that you can confess with Christians everywhere. It's good, though, to also think about your own personal relationship to Christ, about where you are on your faith journey. Please jot down a few of your thoughts about this, whatever they are, positive or negative. If you're still searching for God, please say so. If you've committed your life to Christ, what does it mean to you to be a Christian? You may share your answer with the group or keep it private, as you wish.

Don't Quit

"Stay alert. This is hazardous work I'm assigning you. You're going to be like sheep running through a wolf pack. . . . Don't be naïve. Some people will impugn your motives, others will smear your reputation—just because you believe in me. . . . Don't quit. Don't cave in. It is all well worth it in the end."

—Matthew 10:16ff., *The Message*

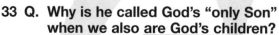

33 Q. Why is he called God's "only Son" when we also are God's children?

A. Because Christ alone is the eternal, natural* Son of God.
We, however, are adopted children of God — adopted by grace through Christ.

* "natural" means that Christ shares the Father's divinity

34 Q. Why do you call him "our Lord"?

A. Because —
not with gold or silver,
but with his precious blood —
he has set us free
from sin and from the tyranny of the devil,
and has bought us,
body and soul,
to be his very own.

How does our membership in God's family differ from Christ's?

How do we become children of God? In other words, what must we do before we can claim God as our Father? See John 1:12 for help.

On a separate sheet of paper, write about how you know (or are uncertain) that you are God's child. How do you know (or why are you uncertain?) See Romans 8:14-17 for help.

Go around the circle and mention one or two good things you experience (or would like to experience) as a member of the family of God.

What do tyrants do? Give an example of one if you can. How can sin be a tyrant?

Go around the circle and give examples of how sins or even too much of a good activity can become tyrants in our lives, taking up our time, energy, and money.

If Jesus has "bought us," then are we his slaves? Why or why not? See Romans 8:15 and John 15:15.

Go around the circle and mention one or two benefits that you experience (or would like to experience) because Jesus is your Lord.

We all struggle against sin. Often we have the best intention of never repeating a particular sin that has been stalking us. When we do it again, we feel guilty, and we find it hard to ask forgiveness for the same sins over and over. Sometimes we feel trapped as if we can't help committing those same old sins. On a separate sheet of paper, write about what you hear Jesus your Lord—the one who sets you free from the tyranny of sin— saying to you in that situation.

GOD'S SON, OUR LORD

<Warm-up>

Your drama team will use a bag of props to put together a quick skit about how busy you are in a typical day. You must use all the props in your skit. You'll have five minutes to get ready. Have fun!

<Main Event>

With others in your group, work through Q&A 33-34, pausing as indicated to

 discuss a question with the whole group whenever you see this symbol

 go around the circle with each person responding whenever you see this symbol

 write a private response on a separate piece of paper whenever you see this symbol

<Follow-up>

What are you personally willing to do this coming week, despite your busy schedule, to recognize Jesus as Lord of every part of your life? Choose one or more of the following, or add your own idea:

■ I recognize that I'm not spending enough time getting to know my Lord. This week I will try to . . .

■ I recognize that there are areas of my life where my other priorities are crowding out my Lord. This week I will make an effort to . . .

■ There are some gray areas of my life where I really don't want Jesus to be Lord because that would put a stop to doing these things. This week I will talk to God about . . .

■ I'm in the process of making Jesus the Lord of my life. This week I want to praise and thank him by . . .

Dialogue

i feel awkward
because it's been so long
since i've been near you.
    i've missed you too;
    i think about you every day.
But i've messed up;
i've done a lot of things
that i regret.
    it's okay, child.
    i forgive you.
i don't understand
i turn away,
i ignore you
    i'm still here
    right beside you.
i try to live without you
even though i know deep inside
that you're still a part of me.
    you don't have to make yourself lovable;
    i love you how you are.
even after everything i've done,

and everything that has happened,
would it offend you if i called you bizarre?
   i am bizarre;
   more so than you'll ever know.
this may seem strange,
but could i please ask you
to hold me, for a little while?
   my child, i've been waiting for you
   with outstretched arms.

—Poem by Janie (not published, copyright 1996)
as it appears in *Dangerous Wonder* by Michael Yaconelli,
© 1998 by Michael Yaconelli. Used by permission of NavPress,
PO Box 35001, Colorado Springs, CO 80935.

**35 Q. What does it mean that he
"was conceived by the Holy Spirit
and born of the virgin Mary"?**

A. That the eternal Son of God,
who is and remains
true and eternal God,[1]
took to himself,
through the working of the Holy Spirit,[2]
from the flesh and blood of the virgin Mary,[3]
a truly human nature
so that he might become David's true descendant,[4]
like his brothers in every way[5]
except for sin.[6]

[1] John 1:1; 10:30-36; Acts 13:33 (Ps. 2:7); Col. 1:15-17; 1 John 5:20
[2] Luke 1:35
[3] Matt. 1:18-23; John 1:14; Gal. 4:4; Heb. 2:14
[4] 2 Sam. 7:12-16; Ps. 132:11; Matt. 1:1; Rom. 1:3
[5] Phil. 2:7; Heb. 2:17
[6] Heb. 4:15; 7:26-27

**36 Q. How does the holy conception and birth of Christ
benefit you?**

A. He is our mediator,[1]
and with his innocence and perfect holiness
he removes from God's sight
my sin—mine since I was conceived.[2]

[1] 1 Tim. 2:5-6; Heb. 9:13-15
[2] Rom. 8:3-4; 2 Cor. 5:21; Gal. 4:4-5; 1 Pet. 1:18-19

LIKE US

\<Warm-up\>

Imagine what it would be like if Jesus were physically present here on earth today, just as he was among the Jews over 2,000 years ago.

■ Where would he live?

■ What would he do for a living?

■ What would he look like?

\<Main Event\>

Sorting Out the Truth About the Incarnation

Use Q&A 35 and your Bibles to decide if the following statements are true or false:

1. _____ When Christ came to earth, he became "one of us" and laid aside his divinity until he returned to heaven.
2. _____ The "Word" in John 1:1 is Jesus Christ.
3. _____ Jesus was simply obeying God the Father's wish that he (Jesus) take on human flesh (check Philippians 2:6-7).
4. _____ The Holy Spirit, not Joseph, made Mary pregnant (check Luke 1:35).
5. _____ Had Jesus been conceived in the normal way, he would not have been sinless.

6. _____ Mary had to be holy and sinless in order for Christ to be holy and sinless.
7. _____ Christ's human nature came from his mother, Mary.
8. _____ For her humble faith and her role as Jesus' mother, Mary deserves our praise.
9. _____ During his time on earth, Christ experienced the full range of human emotions, problems, temptations, sicknesses, failures, fears, and successes (check Hebrews 2:17).
10. _____ Though fully human in every way, Jesus never lied, cheated, hated others, stole, bad-mouthed his parents, wanted what others had, or dishonored God in any other way.

Exploring How This Helps Us

What good does all this do you? That's what the Catechism writers wanted to know. In fact, their very next question asks: "How does the holy conception and birth of Christ benefit you?"

Read answer 36. Then, in the space below, rewrite the answer using your own words and thoughts, making it more personal and letting it express your feelings. You may add other ways that Christ's incarnation helps you as well. Check out 2 Corinthians 5:21; Hebrews 4:15; and Philippians 2:5-6 for additional ideas.

\<Follow-up\>

Choose one or more of the following ways to praise our Lord for what he has done for us in his incarnation:

■ Write a short note or prayer to Jesus expressing your feelings about what he's done for you in coming into our world to be "one of us."

■ Draw a sketch or design that expresses what the incarnation means to you.

■ With one or two others, write a litany of praise to Jesus for all the benefits his incarnation brings us.

■ Look up Mary's song in Luke 1:46-55. With one or two others, make a responsive reading or litany out of this beautiful song. Or, if you prefer, interpret the song with movements/gestures/dance as another person reads it aloud to the class.

God Came Near

She looks into the face of the baby. Her son. Her Lord. His Majesty. At this point in history, the human being who best understands who God is and what he is doing is a teenage girl in a smelly stable. She can't take her eyes off him. Somehow Mary knows she is holding God. *So this is he.* She remembers the words of the angel. "His kingdom will never end."

He looks like anything but a king. His face is prunish and red. His cry, though strong and healthy, is still the helpless and piercing cry of a baby. And he is absolutely dependent on Mary for his well-being.

Majesty in the midst of the mundane. Holiness in the filth of sheep manure and sweat. Divinity entering the world on the floor of a stable, through the womb of a teenager and in the presence of a carpenter.

—*God Came Near* by Max Lucado, © 1987, W. Publishing, a division of Thomas Nelson, Inc. Nashville, TN. All rights reserved. Reprinted by permission.

**37 Q. What do you understand
by the word "suffered"?**

A. That during his whole life on earth,
but especially at the end,
Christ sustained
in body and soul
the anger of God against the sin of the whole human race.[1]

This he did in order that,
by his suffering as the only atoning sacrifice,[2]
he might set us free, body and soul,
from eternal condemnation,[3]
and gain for us
God's grace,
righteousness,
and eternal life.[4]

[1] Isa. 53; 1 Pet. 2:24; 3:18
[2] Rom. 3:25; Heb. 10:14; 1 John 2:2; 4:10
[3] Rom. 8:1-4; Gal. 3:13
[4] John 3:16; Rom. 3:24-26

**38 Q. Why did he suffer
"under Pontius Pilate" as judge?**

A. So that he,
though innocent,
might be condemned by a civil judge,[1]
and so free us from the severe judgment of God
that was to fall on us.[2]

[1] Luke 23:13-24; John 19:4, 12-16
[2] Isa. 53:4-5; 2 Cor. 5:21; Gal. 3:13

**39 Q. Is it significant
that he was "crucified"
instead of dying some other way?**

A. Yes.
This death convinces me
that he shouldered the curse
which lay on me,
since death by crucifixion was accursed by God.[1]

[1] Gal. 3:10-13 (Deut. 21:23)

BY HIS SUFFERING

\<Warm-up\>

■ What examples of human suffering have you seen or heard about recently that have moved you to sympathy or to anger or made you wonder why these bad things happened?

■ Agree or disagree: It's almost impossible to live without experiencing some form of pain or hurt.

\<Main Event\>

1. The Catechism says that Christ suffered at the end of his life but also "during his whole life on earth." Illustrate with a simple sketch and add a caption to one or more of the passages below (as assigned).

   ■ Luke 2:7
   ■ Luke 3:21
   ■ Luke 4:1-2
   ■ Luke 4:16, 28-30
   ■ Mark 3:20-21
   ■ Luke 20:1-2
   ■ Luke 22:47-48

   ■ Mark 14:50-51
   ■ Luke 22:60-62
   ■ Luke 22:63-64
   ■ Luke 23:18-19
   ■ John 19:1-3
   ■ Luke 23:33

2. What specific instances of suffering are mentioned in answers 38-39?

3. Why do you think the Apostles' Creed mentions an obscure Roman judge named Pontius Pilate (see Q&A 38)?

4. Why does the Creed mention that Christ was crucified instead of just saying that he died (see Q&A 39)?

5. Underline those parts of answers 37, 38, and 39 that explain why Christ, the sinless one, suffered.

6. What makes Jesus' suffering different from ours?

<Follow-up>

Your teacher will explain what to do here.

The Curse

"Why, the Catechism asks, is it a big deal that Christ was crucified? The answer is simple. Jesus Christ was cursed, but not by Pilate nor by the Jews who wanted him hung. Jesus Christ was cursed—now take a deep breath, this is the big one—Jesus Christ was cursed by God.

The cross strapped on his shoulders was our sin, which did and does deserve God's curse. . . . God's own Son is cursed with our sin. Here's the good news: by doing that, God freed us to live in love with God forever."

—James C. Schaap, *Every Bit of Who I Am,* page 85

40 Q. Why did Christ have to go all the way to death?
   A. Because God's justice and truth demand it:[1]
   only the death of God's Son could pay for our sin.[2]

[1] Gen. 2:17
[2] Rom. 8:3-4; Phil. 2:8; Heb. 2:9

"Death was the only way for Christ . . . because God is true and God is just. We might add, "and God is love." The only other way would have been death for us who had sinned rather than the curse for him who bore our sin."

—Andrew Kuyvenhoven, *Comfort and Joy,* page 103

41 Q. Why was he "buried"?
   A His burial testifies
   that he really died.[1]

[1] Isa. 53:9; John 19:38-42; Acts 13:29; 1 Cor. 15:3-4

"The writers of the Catechism wanted people to understand there was no question that Jesus really died. In the seventh century, the Koran claimed Jesus didn't die on the cross. Ahmadiya Muslims claim Jesus fled to India, where a shrine in Srinagar, Kashmir, marks his ultimate grave. In the nineteenth century, liberal theologians suggested Christ only fainted on the cross or that he had been given a drug that made him appear to die but later revived in the cool air of the tomb. In 1982, the book *Holy Blood, Holy Grail* claimed that Pilate had been bribed to allow Jesus to be taken from the cross before he was dead. And the myth that Jesus survived the crucifixion continues to circulate."

—Jane Vogel and Mary Sytsma, *Questions Worth Asking*

**42 Q. Since Christ has died for us,
   why do we still have to die?**
   A. Our death does not pay the debt of our sins.[1]
   Rather, it puts an end to our sinning
   and is our entrance into eternal life.[2]

[1] Ps. 49:7
[2] John 5:24; Phil. 1:21-23; 1 Thess. 5:9-10

"The death Christ died was different from our death. His death was a punishment for sin. Ours is no longer a punishment but a narrow door through which we must go to be with the Lord.

The real sting has been taken out of dying . . . but death is still an enemy. It's the last enemy on God's hit list."

—Andrew Kuyvenhoven, quoted in *Questions Worth Asking,* page 167

43 Q. What further advantage do we receive from Christ's sacrifice and death on the cross?

A. Through Christ's death
our old selves are crucified, put to death, and buried with him,[1]
so that the evil desires of the flesh
may no longer rule us,[2]
but that instead we may dedicate ourselves
as an offering of gratitude to him.[3]

[1] Rom. 6:5-11; Col. 2:11-12
[2] Rom. 6:12-14
[3] Rom. 12:1; Eph. 5:1-2

"Could it be any clearer? Our old way of life was nailed to the Cross with Christ, a decisive end to that sin-miserable life—no longer at sin's every beck and call . . . this means you must not give sin a vote in the way you conduct your lives. Don't give it the time of day. Don't even run little errands that are connected with that old way of life. . . . Sin can't tell you how to live."

—excerpts from Romans 5:5-11, *The Message*

44 Q. Why does the creed add, "He descended to hell"?

A. To assure me in times of personal crisis and temptation
that Christ my Lord,
by suffering unspeakable anguish, pain, and terror of soul,
especially on the cross but also earlier,
has delivered me from the anguish and torment of hell.[1]

[1] Isa. 53; Matt. 26:36-46; 27:45-46; Luke 22:44; Heb. 5:7-10

"Hell is a place where God doesn't ring any doorbells, where God's light doesn't shine. Hell is being really alone. Did Jesus Christ suffer that separation? You bet. 'My God, my God, why have you forsaken me?' he said. Hell means being completely forsaken by God; we know Jesus suffered that horrifying loneliness. In that way 'he descended into hell' is absolutely true."

—James C. Schaap, *Every Bit of Who I Am,* page 90

THE DEATH OF DEATH

<Warm-up>

Choose one of the following:

■ Imagine that you have fifteen seconds of prime-time television to say something about death to the American or Canadian public. What would you say?

■ You've been asked to design a billboard about death for a Christian organization. The design should include an illustration of some kind and may include a caption as well.

■ With a partner, pantomime how you think a Christian views his or her own approaching death (one of the partners represents death, the other the Christian).

■ Make a list of five things people fear most about death.

<Main Event>

For each Catechism question and answer you are given, please do the following:

1. Read it over carefully several times.
2. Look up and read the circled passages in the footnotes. Also read the quote next to the Q&A.
3. Rewrite the Catechism's answer in your own words.
4. Write at least one additional thing you wonder about, after thinking over the Catechism's question and answer ("I wonder . . ."). It could be something you don't understand, something you'd like to know more about, or something unusual that interests you.

Q&A 40

Rewritten Catechism answer:

I Wonder . . .

Q&A 41

Rewritten Catechism answer:

I wonder . . .

Q&A 42

Rewritten Catechism answer:

I wonder . . .

Q&A 43

Rewritten Catechism answer:

I wonder . . .

Q&A 44

Rewritten Catechism answer:

I wonder . . .

<Follow-up>

John 19:19 tells us that Pilate had a sign prepared to fasten to Jesus' cross. It read: "Jesus of Nazareth, the King of the Jews." Think back on what you've learned today and use it to write a new statement for Jesus' cross, a statement that means something to you personally. If you prefer, you may draw a symbol that expresses your idea.

**45 Q. How does Christ's resurrection
benefit us?**

A. First, by his resurrection he has overcome death,
so that he might make us share in the righteousness
he won for us by his death.[1]

Second, by his power we too
are already now resurrected to a new life.[2]

Third, Christ's resurrection
is a guarantee of our glorious resurrection.[3]

[1] Rom. 4:25; 1 Cor. 15:16-20; 1 Pet. 1:3-5
[2] Rom. 6:5-11; Eph. 2:4-6; Col. 3:1-4
[3] Rom. 8:11; 1 Cor. 15:12-23; Phil. 3:20-21

ALIVE IN CHRIST

<Warm-up>

Imagine what it must have been like for Jesus' followers to see him again after they had given up all hope. With others in your group, your job is to create a sort of human snapshot (freeze frame) of an encounter between the newly risen Jesus and one or more of his disciples. You'll be assigned one of the following passages to illustrate:

■ John 20:15-16 (Jesus, Mary)
■ John 20:19-20 (Jesus, any number of disciples)
■ John 20:26-28 (Jesus, Thomas, any number of other disciples)
■ John 21:11-13 (Jesus, any number of disciples)

<Main Event>

Resurrection Benefits (Q&A 45)

Our Past

"makes(s) us share in the righteousness he won for us by his death."

■ Read Colossians 1:21-22
■ Express this benefit about your past by completing this statement in your own words:

Because Christ arose, my past is . . .

Our Present

"we too are now resurrected to a new life."

■ Read Ephesians 2:4-6.
■ Express this benefit about your past by completing this statement in your own words:

Because Christ arose, right now, today, I can . . .

Our Future
"Christ's resurrection is a guarantee of our glorious resurrection."
- ■ Read Philippians 3:20-21.
- ■ Express this benefit about your past by completing this statement in your own words:
  Because Christ arose, in the future I will . . .

\<Follow-up\>

Read the letter to you from Paul (on handout). Then go back and underline anything in the letter that you feel speaks directly to you—maybe it's something that encourages you in your new life, maybe it's something that you need to avoid, maybe it's something you need to do or keep on doing.

On the back of the handout write a prayer to Jesus, asking him for help in living your new life. Be as specific in your prayer as you wish. You will be asked to share one line or thought from your prayer, if you wish to do so.

Only Peanuts
"When we start counting blessings, not only children but also mature Christians are inclined to think of health and wealth, the exam we passed, and the car we bought. But such 'blessings' are only peanuts compared to the ones our catechism counts: Jesus lives; therefore
    the past is forgiven,
        the present is meaningful
        and the future is certain!"
—Andrew Kuyvenhoven, *Comfort and Joy,* page 111

84

**46 Q. What do you mean by saying,
"He ascended to heaven"?**

A. That Christ,
> while his disciples watched,
was lifted up from the earth to heaven
and will be there for our good
until he comes again
> to judge the living and the dead.

**47 Q. But isn't Christ with us
until the end of the world
as he promised us?**

A. Christ is truly human and truly God.
> In his human nature Christ is not now on earth;
but in his divinity, majesty, grace, and Spirit
he is not absent from us for a moment.

**48 Q. If his humanity is not present
wherever his divinity is,
then aren't the two natures of Christ
separated from each other?**

A. Certainly not.
Since divinity
> is not limited
and is present everywhere,
it is evident that
> Christ's divinity is surely beyond the bounds of
> the humanity he has taken on,
but at the same time his divinity is in
and remains personally united to
> his humanity.

**49 Q. How does Christ's ascension to heaven
benefit us?**

A. First, he pleads our cause
> in heaven
in the presence of his Father.

"The One who died for us—who was raised to life for us!—is in
the presence of God at this very moment sticking up for us."
—Romans 8:34, *The Message*

"As wonderful as it is to feel all your friends behind you in the very worst of your problems, think how much better it is to know that Jesus Christ the Lord is the real captain of your prayer team."

—James C. Schaap, *Every Bit of Who I Am,* page 97

> Second, we have our own flesh in heaven—
> a guarantee that Christ our head
> will take us, his members,
> to himself in heaven.

"There is plenty of room in my Father's home. If that weren't so, would I have told you that I'm on my way to get your room ready?"

—John 14:2, *The Message*

"Someday we'll see Christ face-to-face in heaven. He's there now, and he guarantees we'll be together in a place so beautiful you won't believe it."

—James C. Schaap, *Every Bit of Who I Am,* page 98

> Third, he sends his Spirit to us on earth
> as a further guarantee.
> By the Spirit's power
> we make the goal of our lives,
> not earthly things,
> but the things above where Christ is,
> sitting at God's right hand.

"And I will ask the Father, and he will give you another Counselor to be with you forever—the Spirit of truth."

—John 14:16-17

50 Q. Why the next words:
"and is seated at the right hand of God"?
A. Christ ascended to heaven,
there to show that he is head of his church,
and that the Father rules all things through him.

"Then Jesus came and said, 'All authority in heaven and on earth has been given to me.'"

—Matthew 28:18

"Forgive us, Lord, for sometimes thinking that you're not in charge. Forgive us our fear. Forgive us our anger. Forgive us for our belief that the world is going to ruin. You're still in charge. Thank you for being the King of Creation."

—James C. Schaap, *Every Bit of Who I Am,* page 99

51 Q. How does this glory of Christ our head benefit us?
A. First, through his Holy Spirit
he pours out his gifts from heaven
upon us his members.

"And his gifts were that some should be apostles, some prophets, some evangelists, some pastors and teachers, to equip the saints for the work of ministry."

—Ephesians 4:11-12, RSV

"Remember these gifts: faith in God, hope that all things will work together for our good, and love for God above all and our neighbors as ourselves. That's how to live. Gifts. From Jesus. Because he rules."

—James C. Schaap, *Every Bit of Who I Am,* page 102

Second, by his power
he defends us and keeps us safe
from all enemies.

"My sheep listen to my voice . . . I give them eternal life and they shall never perish; no one can snatch them out of my hand."

—John 10:28

"Today, the baby in the manger is King of the world. He's in charge. Satan is alive and kicking, but God rules. We don't have to sit in the corner and chew off our fingernails. We don't have to worry endlessly—Christ is King. He's the Lord of our lives, and he rules every inch of this world."

—James C. Schaap, *Every Bit of Who I Am,* page 103

FOR OUR GOOD

<Warm-up>

Ascension Match-up

Ascension Day—a day that the more celebrated holy days like Christmas and Easter often seem to push out of our minds. Just as a way of reminding ourselves what went on at Christ's ascension, play a matching game with some Ascension Day facts. Game details will be explained in class.

<Main Event>

Q&A's 49-51 describe five benefits that you receive from Christ's ascension and place in heaven. They're pretty easy to find, since the Catechism writers actually number them off for you. You can also find a sixth benefit hidden in answer 50.

■ Read through all of the benefits listed in Q&A's 49-51. Pick one of these benefits that you can visualize Jesus doing for you and that makes you feel especially grateful to him.

■ Read the Scripture passage printed next to that benefit, along with any other quotes you find there.

■ Complete this statement: *I hear Jesus saying this to me about what's he doing for me right now in heaven:* (elaborate on the Catechism and biblical statement as you imagine Jesus talking directly to you)
OR

■ Illustrate and write a caption about what you see Jesus doing for you in heaven—be literal or symbolic, as you wish, and, of course, be respectful.

Share your writing or drawing with the group.

<Follow-up>

Write your own prayer of thanks to Jesus for the benefit you worked on in the Main Event section. You'll be given an opportunity to say all or part of your prayer aloud.

**52 Q. How does Christ's return
"to judge the living and the dead"
comfort you?**

A. In all my distress and persecution
I turn my eyes to the heavens
and confidently await as judge the very One
who has already stood trial in my place before God
and so has removed the whole curse from me.[1]
All his enemies and mine
he will condemn to everlasting punishment:
but me and all his chosen ones
he will take along with him
into the joy and the glory of heaven.[2]

[1] Luke 21:28; Rom. 8:22-25; Phil. 3:20-21; Tit. 2:13-14
[2] Matt. 25:31-46; 2 Thess. 1:6-10

DAY OF JUDGMENT

<Warm-up>

Our focus today is the final judgment, the day that the Apostles' Creed says Jesus will return to "judge the living and the dead." Please add your comments about that judgment to the three large sheets of paper posted around your classroom.

<Main Event>

1. The Parable of the Sheep and the Goats (Matthew 25:31-46)

■ On the handout, underline words and phrases that describe unbelievers and what will happen to them on judgment day. Circle words and phrases that describe believers and what will happen to them on judgment day.

■ What is the basis of the judgment that separates the sheep from the goats? How do you square this with the biblical teaching that salvation is by grace, not by works (Ephesians 2:8 and many other passages)?

■ What overall impact does this parable have on you? Why do you think Jesus told it?

2. Q&A 52

■ How do you react to the idea that the final judgment should "comfort you?"

■ The Catechism says that when we are experiencing the troubles of life, we can actually be comforted (strengthened) by thinking of the coming judgment. It gives three reasons for this comfort. Underline the reason that, to you, is most convincing or encouraging. Be ready to explain your choice.

<Follow-up>

Use an index card or slip of paper to jot down a prayer request or concern you have
- about the future (not just the last judgment but anything about the future that concerns you).
- about the oppressed in the world who are waiting for Christ the Judge to set things right at the last judgment.

The (unsigned) cards or slips of paper will be collected, then redistributed so that someone else will pray what you've written.

It's Jesus Sitting There

"What should we think about the future? We should think that it's in God's hands and that we will be well cared for there. We can confidently await Christ's second coming and our final judgment. Why? Because we know Jesus. We saw him when he was lowered to the straw as a human like us. We saw him walk into Pilate's court as the defendant. We saw him when, though found innocent by the court, he was executed for crimes that we committed. And when we stand in the final judgment and look up toward the judge's seat, it's Jesus sitting there. We have nothing to fear. Jesus has gone from the defendant's chair to the judge's bench. He's already found us 'not guilty' on every count."

—"Around the Table," *Landmarks*

**53 Q. What do you believe
concerning "the Holy Spirit"?**

A. First, he, as well as the Father and the Son,
  is eternal God.[1]

  Second, he has been given to me personally,[2]
    so that, by true faith,
    he makes me share in Christ and all his blessings,[3]
    comforts me,[4]
    and remains with me forever.[5]

[1] Gen. 1:1-2; Matt. 28:19; Acts 5:3-4
[2] 1 Cor. 6:19; 2 Cor. 1:21-22; Gal. 4:6
[3] Gal. 3:14
[4] John 15:26; Acts 9:31
[5] John 14:16-17; 1 Pet. 4:14

SPIRIT AT WORK

<Warm-up>

Read "Dialogue" (from the handout) and think about the question at the end. How would you answer it?

<Main Event>

With others in your group, create a poster that shows what the Holy Spirit does in our lives. Use the Bible and Q&A 53 for ideas. Look up the circled Bible passages in the footnotes to Q&A 53 and the additional passages listed below. Then fill your poster with things the Spirit does. For each action of the Spirit that you list, please include a Bible reference in (in parentheses) behind it; for example, "sanctifies us, helps us become more like Jesus" (1 Peter 1:2). Add some simple illustrations to your poster and give it a caption.

Additional passages to check: John 14:26; John 16:7-8; Acts 1:8; Romans 8:16; Romans 8:26; 1 Corinthians 12:3; 1 Corinthians 12:7-11; Galatians 5:22; 1 Peter 1:2.

<Follow-up>

■ Describe a time when you've felt the presence of the Spirit in your life, perhaps in one of the ways shown on the posters or in some other way. For example, maybe you've experienced peace during a difficult time in your life, or maybe you sensed the presence of the Spirit during a youth convention or worship time, or maybe you felt the Spirit moving you toward a healthy change in your attitude toward God or others. Jot your thoughts here:

■ Where do you most need the presence of the Spirit in your life? Again, maybe some of the items listed on the posters suggest a part of your spiritual life that could use some help from the Spirit. Maybe you need encouragement in a specific situation you're facing, or maybe you need to "grow" the fruit of the Spirit, or maybe you want your prayer life to be more meaningful to you. In the space below, jot a short prayer to the Spirit about whatever you sense your spiritual need to be.

Not Without the Spirit

"A sinner can no more repent and believe without the Holy Spirit's aid than he can create a world."

—Charles Spurgeon

**54 Q. What do you believe
concerning "the holy catholic church"?**

A. I believe that the Son of God
   through his Spirit and Word,[1]
   out of the entire human race,[2]
   from the beginning of the world to its end,[3]
gathers, protects, and preserves for himself
   a community chosen for eternal life[4]
      and united in true faith.[5]
And of this community I am[6] and always will be[7]
   a living member.

[1] John 10:14-16; Acts 20:28; Rom. 10:14-17; Col. 1:18
[2] Gen. 26:3b-4; Rev. 5:9
[3] Isa. 59:21; 1 Cor. 11:26
[4] Matt. 16:18; John 10:28-30; Rom. 8:28-30; Eph. 1:3-14
[5] Acts 2:42-47; Eph. 4:1-6
[6] 1 John 3:14, 19-21
[7] John 10:27-28; 1 Cor. 1:4-9; 1 Pet. 1:3-5

**55 Q. What do you understand by
"the communion of saints"?**

A. First, that believers one and all,
as members of this community,
share in Christ
and in all his treasures and gifts.[1]

Second, that each member
should consider it a duty
to use these gifts
   readily and cheerfully
      for the service and enrichment
         of the other members.[2]

[1] Rom. 8:32; 1 Cor. 6:17; 12:4-7, 12-13; 1 John 1:3
[2] Rom. 12:4-8; 1 Cor. 12:20-27; 13:1-7; Phil. 2:4-8

ONE IN THE LORD

<Warm-up>

Please take a moment to jot down one or more prayer requests or reasons for thanks/praise on a slip of paper. These (unsigned) notes will be collected, then redistributed so that someone else will pray what you've written.

<Main Event>

Q&A 54

Remember when you were a little kid and received a Christmas or birthday gift with the warning "assembly required" printed in tiny letters somewhere on the box? Today we're going to form "assembly teams" and see who can put Q&A 54 back together again. Details to be announced.

Q&A 55

1. What two things do all believers have in common?

2. In what ways have members of your congregation helped or served you, your family, or someone you know? Have you or your family had the opportunity of serving others in your church? If so, how?

3. How does the description of believers in Acts 2:42-47 help you understand what Q&A 55 (and 54) are talking about? What characterizes this early Christian community? Would you like your church community today to be like it? Why or why not?

\<Follow-up\>

How do you see the local Christian community of which you are a part? Place an X on the continuum to show your agreement or disagreement:

■ I see my congregation as a true part of God's one worldwide church.

   Agree 5   4   3   2   1 Disagree

■ I appreciate knowing that I will "always be a part" of the worldwide community of believers.

   Agree 5   4   3   2   1 Disagree

■ I sense a real spirit of cooperation and helpfulness in my congregation.

   Agree 5   4   3   2   1 Disagree

■ I feel loved and cared for by the other members of my congregation.

   Agree 5   4   3   2   1 Disagree

■ My gifts are recognized and I'm encouraged to use them to serve others in my congregation and beyond.

   Agree 5   4   3   2   1 Disagree

■ I would like to be more involved in my congregation than I am now.

   Agree 5   4   3   2   1 Disagree

56 Q. What do you believe
concerning "the forgiveness of sins"?

    A. I believe that God,
        because of Christ's atonement,
    will never hold against me
        any of my sins[1]
        nor my sinful nature
            which I need to struggle against all my life.[2]

    Rather, in his grace
        God grants me the righteousness of Christ
        to free me forever from judgment.[3]

[1] Ps. 103:3-4, 10, 12; Mic. 7:18-19; 2 Cor. 5:18-21; 1 John 1:7; 2:2
[2] Rom. 7:21-25
[3] John 3:17-18; Rom. 8:1-2

FORGIVEN

<Warm-up (10 minutes)>

1. Recall something you did that was kind of dumb but made perfect sense at the time. Here are some examples to get you thinking:
   - lit a firecracker with a short fuse
   - bought a car from a friend
   - put your glasses on the floor
   - hid something in a special place, then forgot where
   - left car running, then locked doors while gassing up
   - participated in a hot-dog eating contest
2. What's generally easier for you—to forgive yourself or to forgive others?
3. Why do we often find it hard to forgive ourselves and to accept God's forgiveness?

—Keith Stulp, *29 More Great Bible Studies*

<Main Event (30-35 minutes)>

Bible Study: Speaking of Guilt . . .

- Group 1: Read Matthew 27:1-5. Then create a short skit starring Judas the betrayer. Try to show something of the enormous burden Judas must have carried for what he had done.
- Group 2: Read Matthew 26:69-75. Then create a short skit starring Peter the denier. Try to show something of the enormous burden Peter must have carried for what he had done.

Questions for Discussion

- On a scale of 1 (small sin) to 10 (huge sin), how would you rate Judas's betrayal and Peter's denial?

- Did either of these men repent? If so, do you think Jesus forgave them?
- Judas hung himself and Peter later became the leader of the church. How do you account for the difference?
- What can we learn from these two stories?

Q&A Markup

Answer the questions below by marking as directed the parts of Catechism answer 56 that answer the questions.

1. Why does God forgive us? (underline)
2. What two things does God forgive? (circle)
3. How does God forgive? (wavy underline)
4. When does God refuse to forgive a believer's sin? (rectangle)
5. God "subtracts" our sins and then "adds" something to us. What? (plus sign at end of line)
6. What's the bottom line for us? (double underline)
   What do you personally find most comforting/encouraging about answer 56? Write your response here.

<Follow-up>

Details to be announced.

When You're Hit with Guilt

"When we commit heinous—and not-so-heinous—acts against others, sometimes we carry a huge burden of guilt with us for years afterward. Every time we remember the event, we burn with shame. We beat ourselves up over these incidents. 'Why was I stupid enough to do *that*?' we ask ourselves again and again. Some of us would gladly give up just about anything if we could just undo one truly dumb thing we said or did to somebody. . . . When you're hit with guilt and have trouble forgiving yourself, remember this: As a child of God, your actions may be bad, but you are not. Don't equate, 'I'm a sinner' with 'I'm a horrible person.' If you need to, stand in front of a mirror and say, 'God forgives you and so do I.' Every time that troubling incident comes to mind, remind yourself that you are God's *forgiven* child. The Bible says, 'If we confess our sin, he is faithful and just and will forgive us our sins' (1 John 1:9)."

—Keith Stulp, *29 More Great Bible Studies*

1. **Where** will your soul go when you die?

2. **When** will this happen to your soul?

5. **Why** can your dead, decayed body be raised and reunited to your soul? What makes this possible?

57 Q. How does "the resurrection of the body" comfort you?

3. **What** will happen to your body?

A. Not only my soul
  will be taken immediately
    after this life
  to Christ its head,[1]
but even my very flesh, raised by
    the power of Christ,
  will be reunited with my soul
  and made like Christ's
    glorious body.[2]

[1] Luke 23:43; Phil. 1:21-23
[2] 1 Cor. 15:20, 42-46, 54; Phil. 3:21; 1 John 3:2

6. **What** will your new body be like?

4. **When** will this happen to your body? (This question isn't answered by the Catechism. Please check 1 Corinthians 15:51-52.)

7. **Who** (besides you) is this all about?

8. **So what?** **What** part of this Q&A do you find most comforting or hopeful?

1. **Who** is this Q&A about?

2. **When** do you and all believers begin to experience the joy of eternal life?

5. **Where** will all this blessedness be experienced? (This one isn't answered by the Catechism. Please check Revelation 21:1-2.

58 Q. How does the article concerning "life everlasting" comfort you?

A. Even as I already now
    experience in my heart
    the beginning of eternal joy,[1]
so after this life I will have
    perfect blessedness such as
        no eye has seen,
        no ear has heard,
        no human heart has ever
            imagined:
a blessedness in which to praise
        God eternally.[2]

[1] Rom. 14:17
[2] John 17:3; 1 Cor. 2:9

3 **What** will you experience after you die? (mentioned twice)

4. **Who** now living can describe the "perfect blessedness" we will experience after this life?

6. **What** will we be doing in heaven?

7. **So what? What** part of this Q&A do you find most comforting or hopeful?

LIFE EVERLASTING

<Warm-up>

Imagine your life as a timeline. On a separate piece of paper, draw a line to represent your life. Enter your birth date at the left side of the line. Now divide the line into ten equal segments, each representing ten years of your life. Along the line enter two or three important dates from the past—events from your life that have a special meaning to you (moving to a new home; starting a new school; taking a special vacation; getting your first job) Try to include one event that made you very happy.

Now look at the part of your timeline that represents the future. Of course we have no way of knowing what will happen in the future. We just leave that in God's hands. So speculate a bit—enter two or three or more events that you are looking forward to in your future. Take a guess at approximately when they could happen.

Finally, enter a date for your death (if you think the Lord will return before you die, you can guess when that might be).

<Main Event>

1. Fact Web

Journalists often try to answer these questions when digging out the facts for an article: Who? What? When? Where? Why? So what? Read the questions scattered around Q&A 57-58, then circle the part of answers 57 and 58 that answers those questions. Draw lines from the journalism questions to the circled answers to create a "fact web" around each Q&A.

2. What the Bible Says about Heaven

Read Revelation 21:1-11, 22-27. What does this passage say will *not* be present on the new earth? What *will* be present?

3. Back to the Future

Return to the timeline you began earlier and add the events that you learned about in today's session. Of course, there are no dates to attach to these events, so just write them on a new line beneath the first one you drew.

<Follow-up>

We'll be remembering persons we know or know of who have gone to be with the Lord. Details to come.

How Do You Picture Heaven?

"Many of us have a small gallery of pictures of heaven. We have, perhaps, a few pictures of angels and clouds and harps. Maybe God and Christ on thrones are pictures in our gallery. Possibly we imagine gleaming gold streets and a population of heavenly residents quite a lot like ourselves. We have pictures of church-going and hymn singing and resting. All of it is airy and high up and, to tell the truth, somewhat boring and unreal to us.

"It's time to . . . replace those pictures with others. . . . For in Revelation 21 John suggests that the new heaven and new earth will be right here where we now live. Heaven descends to earth, *this* earth. This earth will be purified and renewed so that heaven can be on-site where we now live."

—Cornelius Plantinga, Jr., *A Sure Thing*